PASSAGE

The Wesleyan Poetry Program: Volume 81

PASSAGE

by W. R. MOSES

Wesleyan University Press

MIDDLETOWN, CONNECTICUT

PS
3525
08615
P3

2/1976
Am. Lit. Cont.

Acknowledgement is gratefully made to the following periodicals, in the pages of which a number of the poems in this book were first published: *American Weave, Approach, Denver Quarterly, Epos, The Georgia Review, Kansas Quarterly, little review of the pacific northwest, The Massachusetts Review, The New York Times, Northeast, Poetry Northwest, The University Review* and *The Wascana Review.*

The publisher gratefully acknowledges the support of the publication of this book by The Andrew W. Mellon Foundation.

Library of Congress Cataloging in Publication Data

Moses, William Robert, 1911–
    Passage.

    (The Wesleyan poetry program: v. 81)
    I.   Title.
PS3525.08615P3   811'.5'4   75-33361
ISBN 0-8195-2081-0
ISBN 0-8195-1081-5 pbk.

Manufactured in the United States of America
First edition

To
E. and E. again,
again with love.

CONTENTS

I

MORNING ABOVE A NEW DAM

Jump, little new-planted fish,
Get a look at the low east. Flight
Of early teal that come down plump
By maize stalks standing in newly spread
Water, stare east. It will not look
Dead, no-color, this barely morning
Sky, to the likes of you and you;
But not-yet color. The promises
Of orient will comfort the eye
Of fish that can swim, duck that can fly.

Sad, dark, forever unlooking:
That is your best way, bushes
That stand in new water. No glad
Colors can preinform your view,
Who cannot move; a never-again
Hue, for drowning bushes, the sky.
Blue it will not be any more.

I, of course, may look wherever
I please; and the migrating flock
Of redwinged blackbirds that vie
For perch on nearly each twig
Of wet-foot sunflowers, wherever.
Big with promise of a really new
Sun is the east; conveniently dark
To permit a little more sleep
The zenith. When day is really begun,
We, independents, will have fun.

Red, though, so red, scarlet
As flowing blood, each redwing's shoulder
Patch. In me, a small dread,
Patch-size, product of morning cold
And strangeness, perhaps. May we be
Bold for the day, the birds and I?
Small my fear; just inch-big

The patch. And yet death's entrance wound
May be no bigger, nor shall we forestall
That; but it will pierce us all.

SALUTE

I went hunting along up the side of the reservoir.
It was public hunting area, government land
Apportioned to the loves of the heart, to certain of the loves
Of the bloody old anarch heart. I found where a town
Had been, some scrap of a town. A retaining wall
Curbed a hillside yet; there was even a planted line
Of tough iris, frost-dimmed, crowded by weeds.
There was even a sidewalk, nearly overarched by weeds.
Comment was pointless: most of man's artifacts
Are already deeper in words than they are in dust.
When I fired at something, the 20-gauge rang a bell.

THE DAY OF THE DOG

The dogs of hell
Are dangerous, aren't they? Cerberus
Made Dante wince enough.
And don't you feel
How dreadfully met would be
The doleful Scandinavian monster Garm,
That doorkeep of the frosty underground?

It is sunlit morning here by the reservoir
And the heat-struck ice responds with
The usual booms. But sometimes there is a rushing of
Whines and yelps, as though one heard the resounding
Cries of gigantic puppies, trying recklessly
To climb from the nest, get out and reach the world.

Now who did what,
Now who reshaped heedlessly
The well made, sane earth
And wakened to breed and feed
The whelps of hell, the greedy, dangerous powers?
And when will they be here,
Here, where they are coming?

OF LEECHES ET AL.

I

We had lifted out the canoe from the creek
And set it on top of the car.
As I fiddled with a cord, the bow fastening,
I saw we had acquired a figurehead
Of sorts, a little bloodsucker, a leech.
He had good hold of aluminum
Canoe-skin with one end; the other he stretched
In leech's movement, rather sinuous
And graceful, trying for a useful grasp
On the air. He was never going to get that,
Of course, never, never going to get that.

II

Leeches can have really vicious bad luck.
One of us shook off his lure,
The other day, one of those tack-toothed devourers,
A pike. His latest devouring
Was a leech. In the crisis of getting caught
He regurgitated the crippled
Little brute, and left him stuck as though baited
On the hard-steel, flesh-holding barbs
Of the gang hook. What a truly godawful
Exchange that was!

III

I keep recalling, though I'd rather not,
Those newspaper pictures of rigorous
Doings by mushrooms, or maybe daffodil
Bulbs, when, tough and undaunted,
They rough their claim to lebensraum upward
Right through the dead repression
Of asphalt paving. It's no good announcing

A triumph of life almighty
In happenings like that. The next shuffling heel,
Whirring wheel, will hurl down
Smashed, those brave ones. A plague, a plague!

THE CAT WAR

At the foot of the sloping alley
A storm sewer, the home,
Until she shall die or move,
Of a stray cat. She sits
On the barred-over ledge of the sewer
And watches me, who sit
In the fenced backyard of a house,
My home till I move or die.

It is she who tests our balance:
In neat quiet, goes creeping
Under the fence and into
Some bushes, no doubt to hunt.
To me her meat, the birds,
Are not meat but something
I anti-hunt, with water
Year round, and seeds in the snow.
I rout her, and back she scats
To her ledge and sits waiting.

Triangular tab-face, I do
Like her; the only thing
Is, those birds. And she
Does have to be cautious, but
Adds to her wary stare
No fear I can see, or dislike.
I could tame her: sweet-talk
And saucers of milk would do it.
We could set up a loving household.
But then, what about those birds?

Sitting on chair and ledge,
We perch, it appears, on the poles
Of a dialectic we didn't
Invite, in an equilibrium
Of remarkably sterile purity

AS THOUGH

As though there were a catch of stuff,
Bark scraps maybe, bits of dead leaf, de
And scum and slime, a dirty cover for s
It heaves slightly, up and down pluck a
Eddies, trembles, hesitates
Toward becoming heavier, thicker, mo
Toward thinning, dispersing, breaking
Opaque trash with motion beneath it.

And as though out of cold, clean san
There bubbled that coldest and clear
That oldest water of the world pristi
It works in the dark, wavering,
Rising, rising in a writhing of grace
Working up, up,
Pushing to extend, to force to the l
Struggling against a dark somewh

As though
A random dead cover released
Bits of itself to sink, clogging an
For the prevalence of deadness a
But the live, limpid bubbles cam
To shove off the settling fragme
To break up and end the dark c
Rising and sinking, sinking an

In which we know that if things
Were different, things would be different.
God knows what power of explosion
Can build itself in the stillness
Of balances fixed as this one.
Bless you, cat, go away!

IN THE NORTH WIND

There they are, the long wings pumping,
The strong necks straight, declaring direction.
There they are, but not: There they go.
Thoughtless feathers, or unlucky feathers,
Careless what field they fed in, or maybe
Having no choice what field they fed in,
They are high south now from the open water
In the refuge, and even Canada geese
Can not fly north into this north wind.
They sideslip east, hunting for an eddy;
And sideslip west, hunting for an eddy.
They pump and pump, declaring direction.
They can't declare it as long as the wind can.
Willing what they must, they turn, ride south
To the luck or the unluck in the wide south,
Some other refuge, or maybe no refuge.

THE BAT

And then, with the other debris,
This bat, he also well smashed
By the hail. With killed leaves,
Birds, flowers, he lay on his back
And showed a white wing bone to morning.
He had life enough in him to hiss disapproval
Of things as they were. So,
I would have to kill to be kind, eh?
Boot heel or spade edge. But then,
Reachably low, I noticed a hollow
In a big old tree. And tumbled the bat into it,
And he fell down out of my eye-reach, forever.
The answers are dark, dark in a hollow tree.

A RUNNING FIGURE

Memory—for the sake of a metaphor,
Call it a kaleidoscope. I wish it contained more pieces.
Some patterns recur too often, some bad ones—

A running figure: as focus grows certain,
I see it is just past babyhood, with terrifying softness
In cheeks, terrifying gentleness in eyes.
Whether impelled by a bell, or by herd impulse,
It strains, in the midst of vague figures,
Toward a dark building, high, very grimy.
The sky over it is dark, very grimy.
Cinders or paving underfoot, dark, very harsh.

The bad joke of it: with the eyes of my flesh
I never once saw this infuriating pattern
With so much darkness grating in toward the center.

BERRY PICKER

That old white-head, having managed to find
A blackberry patch thorning a rocky hill,
Drives out, time after time, in the kind of car
That has status glinting silvery from its chrome
To a harvest he needn't make. I think that, surprised,
Some year he suddenly knew that the way to love
His God to the highest power was simply to love
Vegetable creation: with each pluck of a fruit
He praises God. Regardless, his face
Is sour, as though with unripeness, as though it seems
Terribly long till the sweet apotheosis
When every slip and scratch is obliterated
In the tangible presence of the glowing, eternal Berry.

YOUNGER TO OLDER

Fortunate I don't have to give you a label.
Little belief I'd get, calling you a tiger,
Topped as you are with Hera-like cow eyes,
Exhaling a meadowy breath like cowslips.
Carnivore! I know the corpses you eat.

Not me, by the hardest.
Hurling rocks, I slow your advance.
Ardently I scramble a rock-face that you can't climb.
Contemptuously I scoot to another part of the forest, and stay there.

That's life, that's history.
Here you are, now, almost monkey-wrinkled,
With hands slowly lifting to shell-frail temples.
Trying to be tender, I help you from a pew;
Protectively I support you toward the communion rail.

AUTUMN: BEFORE LEAVING

"You will be a respected man where you are going,"
My blood sang me gaily; "the jargon, you will learn it;
As for any insignificant jealousy or skepticism,
You will smile it down or spurn it.
There is choice of places—far, of course, yet easy to reach,
And civic and aesthetic pleasures in each."

But something—shrinkage of blood with the cold come?—
Dismays me worse than the most enormous distance.
What fire I have built it is necessary I crouch by,
Too little, too lacking persistence
To go where surely the people are too malicious
For me to contend with, who am only weak and not vicious.

As soon as I can, I shall set up my best head
As oracle (my brows down in sober reflection,
My cheeks furrowed a little, my eyes level),
And submit it the question;
But how disquieting if I am unable to discover
Whether I am checked merely by a cold rain in October!

DECLINE OF THE WEST

Man, who once could tickle the angels' toes,
From the gorilla to the white ant he goes.

SHRUG

I am reading, suspiciously, *Sports & Recreation.* . . .

Ah, but I know, have known, not to advantage,
Too many kneaded waters where no man's knack
Shall waken fins to their feeding except, say, on Wednesday
Alternate weeks. Flabby the lakes, lacking freshness,
Larruped to death by the bellowing dashing of bull-lined
Deafening speedboats. But no, here is no drawback
To a landlord's building a photo file fit to bedizen
A fat-ad. mag. Ten snapshots per summer will fix it,
And forget blank summers no snapshots could possibly fiddle.

Surely I could mount a moral, but who is too stupid
To mock-up a version for himself? Here this month,
Hovering in the backyard idly, iris with sharp heads
Igniting from the green, I saw that the groups in the
Row were gapped widely, wealth dotted too gauntly
To widen the eyes much. Manoeuvering, I walked
Maybe eighty degrees, and dazzling bunched color was modeled,
Of course. Did it backward, and broke the design
Down, broke it to backward, gaunt dotting, of course.

DOG: HER VACATION

Panope the Labrador, lithe-black, sweet-patient,
Rode far wearily, wistful in the rocking car.
The whirligig car breeze, whining over blacktop,
Brought mere pepperings, broke bits piecemeal,
Of the pretty smells of earth, not easy to put in place.
But the trip ended finally. Heady, full of emphasis,
In flowed odors, sharp from the flesh of occupants,
Objects there, in near woods, or private in the wet,
Waste, secret swamp tufts where a dog could run
From sunrise clear to purple night, while people fished shorelines.
The party went on monthlong. Then the pure monotony
Of many roads driven over, miles back to home's door.
Dustily now the query rises, was it really well done
So to rinse the being, burden the responses,
With a bright new treasure, a new brand of treat,
That a dog can only whine over, done now, withheld now?

SURFACE FISHING

I am a fisherman casting
On the charming lake at the charming hour
When the sun is newly set
Though the light is little diminished yet.
I make parabolas with my surface plug
That is meant to counterfeit a swimming frog.

I am pleased well enough
With light and things in the half sphere
I breathe in: the early nighthawk,
The closing lilies, the late flock
Of goldfinches I hear while "Pop!" and "Glug!"
Exclaims my frittery, fussing surface plug.

Yet why should I be constrained
To have, know, only those pretties
That live in *up* and *across*?
I tire of being so long at a loss
For what is *down, under.* My podgy plug
Works hard at being a succulent swimming frog.

I want the nervous splash
Of the dark-muscled power from below
Rising to take my lure.
I want to have it, to eat its pure
Strength. Shall I change, let some other enticement fall?
For nothing comes up, nothing comes up at all.

PASTORAL

Everyone knows
The marks of pastoral with its petals falling—
Cold rock, cold air, cold grass;
The fish rebellious: the stringer empty. . . .

The cold child with a cold coming on
Knew them. But warmed himself
With a phantasy of order: a warmed room
And pages neat with numbers: the arithmetic
Learned in his months at school.
The wild river was welcome to its wild fish.
But warm pages neat with controlled numbers. . . .

That was a long, long time ago.
Who controls what? The world smothers in numbers.
Will it not be spring by the river
And the buds swelling?

FROM THE HEART OF DARKNESS

You ought to see the way
I have learned to deal with the tsetse fly,
The leech, the hookworm, the mamba!
In the forty years of my stay
We have grown to be friends, nearly,
Or at least respectful enemies, harmless.

Note how my skin (unmarked
By thorn, or tooth, or any disease—
I've stopped those, stood them off)
Is the right-colored skin to please
These shark-toothed bipeds, my buddies,
Who follow me, greet me, know all about me!

Of course. I earn my keep
In ways that mark me the easy master
Of tribal know-how.
Many a fellow can sleep
Full-bellied because I taught him
Right use of the snare, the fishhook, the bow.

And yet I do not brag.
In fact, this list is too musty, too boring
To continue. Remoter memories
Keep nudging me. (I can afford it.
I have this present so leashed,
Muzzled, claw-clipped, I needn't be watching.)

Where is it cool? Where
Is the water icy? The May flower blooming?
Where is it needless to practice
Hypocrisy and fraud to evade
Violence? In short—hadn't I a home?
More and more these matters concern me, who crouch
By jungle game paths, deadly with my killing spear.

FUNERAL TRIP

I

Sunday evening, middle downtown.
Damn it, does no one eat in this town
On Sunday evening? Hurrying cold, we go
Past locked restaurant doors, and the glow
Of night-lights in windows. Sometimes the head
Of a clothing store dummy, appearing waxy-dead,
Inclines to us. Hunger, shadows, the night wind grow
Stronger. No pedestrians. We walk alone.

And had damn well better be careful to walk
Entirely on the empty, gritty sidewalk.
The life, at least the movement, snarls down every street:
Four lanes of traffic. Its beat
Is fast, the usual hurrying *to*
From. As though there were speedway traffic through
Pompeii, and in pointless surprise one had to see it
As he walked with the dead, block by block.

II

Forenoon here, a kind of dull
Cloudlight-smokelight. Limestone, sandstone
Of church, courthouse have a soot tone,
Dirty smoke tone God ought to cull
Out of the world's colors. In this
Near downtown the remnant black trees
Are broken, grey fences broken. We wheeze
The smog; some locomotives hiss
Nearby agreement. All this stuff
Is thoroughly familiar. In no way comprehensible.

Well, dirty mixed life requires the best
Language to clean, arrange it. We know
(Don't we?) symbol is the strongest foe

Of the chaotic. So, I snatch for the most
Apt controlling emblems for this poor place
—And what are these sticky in my head
But images of filthy stone, of dead
Trees, of smog acrid in the face?
I could grow terrified at what the town and I are doing.
If a sunbeam shows, I'll ride it out of town.

III

Nice lawn here, rather,
Even though gone grey for winter.
I could admire it
Except that I fish out of memory
An old chart of this sliver
Of land in the near suburbs,
And identify the quince tree here,
And the gooseberry bush there,
And the reeling, overburdened arbor
Of Concord grapes down the middle.
And so I will not admire.
A plague on our pother
Over having nice grass.
May it all be crabgrass!

IV

To interpolate the obvious: of course it is useless
Trying to evade the obvious pain
Of the useless city by pulling out of town
Five miles. Of course people try. Our own
Friends: that would have been a charming home
On the knoll where beeches and oaks reached down
To protect, not smother, and sootless grass
Looked tawny warm, even against snow.
That fancy was before I-70 came through.
Just fancy warmth or protection on the windswept,
Dirty, gritty, abrasive concrete!

Just fancy how soon spilled blood would turn
To ice on that!

V

Our worn room in the slumping old hotel
Tall in the city but not aspiring now
Is good enough house-room. (We'll not be here
Two years from now, or next year,
When the wreckers get it. It's warm now.)

Glass and distance, combined, make pleasant enough
The rusty roofs and a sky like grey snow.
It's casually pleasant to watch the street
Way down, where the harmless cars beat,
And now grow dim under actual snow.

But something is wrong. This is not blizzard country,
Yet look at the snow, how it rides the horizontal wind!
It would look all wrong on a Christmas card,
Where the fat white is never jarred
From patient branches by rude wind.

No, not wrong, right. Christmas calls indoors,
In to an old rich aura in a firm house.
It is right the weather be focused wrong
For Christmas; we'd not be making our long
Trip, were there still such a house.

II

FIGURES IN SNOW

Other kids told me
That young nuns who lived
In that big, mysterious house where nuns lived
Came out, winter nights under moonlight,
To slide on toboggans
Down the slope in front of their house:
Black, improbable joy-shapes over snow
That carried in daylight our humdrum skis.

On brushy vacant ground
Behind the big house
I sometimes walked searching the snow, finding runways
Of rabbits, and interrupting their flow
With snares of fine wire:
Eager out there playing wilderness
With the normal love-and-death contradictions.
I didn't know how to go about it; killed nothing.

Rabbits did run, though,
In dark nights or moonlit.
One morning, tough Arctic trapper on his trapline,
I came to the broken remnant
Of a weak copper snare
—A straightened bare end holding nothing.
I couldn't tell whether the struggle had been easy
Or death-hard. But something went free where it was going.

IN SUPERIOR, LOOKING NORTH

A railway cut off the heel of the bay
As a knife cuts the heel of a loaf.
There is very good flavor in crusts. . . .

Catch it right, catch it just right,
And nothing disposes of winter so well
As migrating song sparrows singing
In willow, by water just open,
Under the pelt and putter of a snow squall
Too late to be anything but innocent.
Music of angels, wild bush angels!
And then it is warm at last,
And at last you put in your fishline. . . .

Qualify, certainly.
Rolling stock had rolled over the legs
Of two different guys I knew
Who got too casual, train-hopping.
That harvest I never connected
With the railroad dick who came huffing and snarling
At us little bastards, we couldn't fish there. . . .

Thereafter we ducked from adults.
But the pardon I need is for keeping so many
Of the little gold, black-barred fish
That would bite by dozens, by hundreds.
They were very small perch. But real perch. . . .

"I used to go hunting with this Indian,
And when he got a moose, he would leave the head in a tree.
That was like for luck; if you didn't do it,
Word would get round to the other moose
You weren't a good fella; you wouldn't do so well.

"I knew the guy well, we were friends,
And he was educated, had the equivalent of grade 12 education,
So I used to kid him:
'You don't really go for that old stuff, do you,
An educated man like you?'

"He wouldn't say much, but he wouldn't back down,
Just, 'Well, every time I go hunting I get a moose;
It can't do any harm'. Kind of grin at me."

In spruce-green heaven
Indian and moose walk formally together,
Or bow to each other in grave respect.

THE HUNTERS IN CABIN 2

There is a sucking, plucking, blubbering gurgle
That bubbles in blood out. Pinkish obscenity
Of moist, broken bone-ends unfleshed.
Sick, jinking forelegs drawing a body
With hind legs broken. There is malodor
Of dishonorable death: bowel-shot, bladder-shot.

Flesh-caught, shall our lives be harmony
Without violence: two sweet colors merging?
Where life is exchange of protein? Where
This is my body that was given for you; eat?

Yet—those with thick bodies who go out before morning
Armed, no matter for frost, no matter for rain:
Their reddened skin is touched with at least the false dawn
Preceding the light eternal.

THE MEDITATION OF A MAN IN A BOAT, C.1910

Wasn't I a rich man's son?
I should have lived in the town
Where, smiling golden, the bank would have known me,
And, smiling perhaps not so golden, the town would have known me.
With coordinates like that, I too would have known me.
Lush green, my lawns would have flourished in the sun.
My father died poor.

If my own projects had prospered
I should have erected a house
Firm on a point strong in the shining
Of this sweet lake, where, known to the sense of the place,
And to far-shore farmers come out for their cows,
I'd have known me well, a maker in a good place.
The point stands empty.

In my boat I sit in the dark
With a line descending to the bullheads
That twitch it; but I doubt that their hunger is knowledge.
Shadows barely deeper than the shadows nighting the bank
Come something—I think wolves, to drink. In doubt,
They prick ears toward me, wondering. I bless them.
I need not know me.

DARK AND DARK

Slowly now, and softly now, and sweetly
The earth in its spin carries us into communion
With the big darkness set with its dancing stars.
The small lights of the small, nearby darkness
Come on, house lamps and street lamps. But trees and hedges
Block and confuse them. My yard, like the rolling sky,
Has just enough light to declare darkness' identity.

I think of the nested thrasher out in the fence,
Closely enfolding her eggs in the grassy structure
Established between wire mesh and the thrusting limbs
Of the old wild grape that scrambles and sprawls so broadly
That it takes from the fence its nature of thin uprightness,
And makes it suggest, in the dark, some primitive longhouse,
Or perhaps an extended burial mound. I wonder

Whether the darkness enfolding the bird's awareness
Is the big darkness that dwarfs the innumerable stars,
Or only the little darkness of the fussy crust
Of earth, that is always fretting to increase the number
Of its little lights, as though it could thus deny
What lies all around it. I think that a being of the wild
Must retain the wild in its heart, however surrounded

By all the pretensions of tameness. It feels the big dark.
Grape leaves are broad; the beams of the small lights strike them
Like weak, stray arrows that glance from impervious shields.
The trunk of a hackberry rises as broad as a hill
To shelter a bird from everything lying beyond it.
The dark that contains the stars, and renders them tiny,
Contains too the bird, softly and sweetly enfolds her.

There was another man lived in the north,
The degree of north we rhyme, nearly, with death.
I'll look at his legacy of images now,
Those he left me, the ones that persist.
The persistent may be important in a land of snow.
There are three pictures of food, only one of death.

Human death, I mean, and that only routine:
The familiar one of the unwary slob who had been
In the town saloon, and then started to plough
To his shack in the woods, but sat down for a nice rest
In the nice moonlight at routine 40 below.
In the morning they found a nice statue of what he had been.

There's more zest, I think, in a picture of the habits
Of another shackman of the woods. He ate rabbits
In quantity, apparently. Daily hunting, though,
Was a nuisance. He would shoot a lot, hang them
Skinned, frozen pure, on his house wall, ready to go
When wanted. You could tell his house by the drapery of rabbits.

One fall some lunacy afflicted a bluejay.
He stayed when the other jays flew away
South. It is shivery-triumphant picturing how
He would hop town streets, finding scraps of peanut
Or other stuff eating people had dropped to blow
Where they happened to. Come spring, he was healthy as if he had
    been away.

Finally, this. My legator liked to eat
Snow-cold apples, but take the edge off the sweet
By adding to his bites little pieces of raw
Orange peel. There was a contrast, the tropic color and tang
Mixed with the northern sweetness, death-colored as snow!
Apparently it left him as much as he needed of the sweet.
Only by mixture, maybe, can you really bring out sweet.

43

A SMALL REPARATION

Oversexed sprawler in alleys;
The bird of love untuned, got dirty;
Frayed little rag in the tail of the city kite—
We all know the English sparrow.
He will not lift our hearts.
He is only grit in the system—harmonious with nothing.

Today I am alone in the snow
Except for four birds coming.
Wind friends, their rising, subsiding
Make graceful wind-ripples visible.
They pick out the snow by contrast,
Its white the whiter for their brown.
They light now, and make little flutters
For the seeds of protruding wild grass;
In the land, off the land living
Like horned larks, or snowflake snow buntings.

God bless us, they are English sparrows.

THE PERFUME OF THE SPHERES

Too late or dull, my blunted ears
Have never heard the singing spheres
Pythagoras heard. In recompense,
I gratify a lower sense.
Whenever late September's breeze
Goes raking in black walnut trees,
Spherical nuts come thudding down.
Their coarse hulls turn the fingers brown,
But give the nose such pungent fact
As a distiller might extract
From twenty kinds of sunny weeds
Mingled. If heavenly sound recedes,
If heaven is now a silent room,
Down here, at least, is spheres' perfume.

BULLHEAD LAKE

Small fish swimming
In the shallows of a woods pond. . . .

One had a malformed tail
And one a jammed neck; looked humpbacked.

They cruised in a lovely small sheet
Lacking inlet or outlet or depth
For margin of safety in winter.
In the bad ones, there was always winterkill.
Whatever was left could start over.

How do I know whether fish triumph?
They functioned;
And I was happy, and loved them.

DREAM

The figure tells me, "I hurt myself.
There was so damn much bleeding. . . ."
It clings to me, leans on my chest, wanting comfort.
My belly goes hollow with sympathy, cold with anger.
I would do anything to erase the hurt.
But I feel my head,
And my head feels orange, sweaty, round as a pumpkin,
With jack-o-lantern mouth laughing,
And it laughs out the silliest damned ineptitude:
"How do you know?"
I'd like to smash the fool pumpkin face,
Like to go down into me to the rusted valves
And hammer them, hammer them open,
So what is inside me could flow.
What's there would be balm, would be medicine.
It would cure that hurt.

AUGUST, LAKE OF THE WOODS

I

The hand of the shriveling prisoner in his dungeon
Reaching through bars for the water out of his reach
—No, of course not. But I feel the stretch
Of secret roots down a rock slope covered too thinly
With earth, for the last, least undryness, and only
Finding more dryness. The sun, you could say, has won.
The birch leaves above those roots have become sun-
Color. They are very lovely, the most charming
Incongruity of color, congruity still of shape,
With green leaves near them on lucky trees rooted deep.

Some losers are fiercely open about their trouble.
Many an island pine has been heaved by the wind
Down; all the high, feathery grace
Without grace sprawled, flattened, skinned.
Wherever that happened, look what the roots have done:
Hauled right out, for the inspection of anyone,
A root-clutch of soil, to show how poor, meagre,
Thin it was, clipped weakly to unhelpful rock.
Sometimes they have hauled out a big slab of rock;
That wasn't good enough either, when things got serious.

II

The poor old assaulted water:
How pieces from above, from the smug air,
Keep poking and altering, probing and shoving it!
Sometimes propellers of active outboards
Will pour it all of a swirl, a dizzy twining.
Sometimes paddles, or ambling dull oars,
Will punch deep, angling and dipping and jabbing.
Bright plastic lures, armed mean with steel hooks,
Come plump down against it, and sinuously bore it.

48

Well, up here there are acrobatic, tough pike;
Hook one, he's likely to air his pugnacity
Like a bass or salmon. And now, plunge,
Yank! I *have* hooked one. Agile, no prudence,
He flares from the surface. Abruptly I picture
What he's really like, the avid, high-pressure
Leanness—a club the angry lake plunks
Hard against air, and leaves it all pulsing;
And against my vision, and leaves it all pulsing.

III

It's an old, old concern: emptiness that isn't empty.
Cavemen side-squinting into the dark; soldiers
Side-squinting into the dark. . . .
                                        Now, this water
Opaque in the cliff's shadow—is it heart-certain
No fangs can rip from it? Is it sure no force
That animates granite can slam down a cliff-chunk
On trespassing heads?
                            —These are just exercises
In atavism; they pall; they don't last long.
But now, from the cliff top, from brush we can't see
Comes a crash, a big crash, perfectly here and authentic.
The dog, by her angry fear, declares *bear.*
But we can't see. We wait; only silence.
We wait; only silence—but what an odd silence!

IV

Amorousness? Greediness?
I don't think either. But see our dog
Kiss, kiss, and again kiss
The scales of these two fish that sag
On a stringer: our noon provision:
The walleyes we have kept for lunch.

49

And see her hover cheek by jowl
With me who crackle twigs for fire.
Now she leans close to the ritual
Of knifing fillets from the bone.
What can such eagerness require
For satisfaction, for relief?

I'll never know. Composure comes.

I watch excitement sublimate
Into the dignity, repose,
Of a sculptured black Egyptian cat
I saw in some museum once:
The dog sits, staring with zircon eyes
Toward wave and tern and island line.

V

Slow gases now expand as smoke
Above the cabin chimney; good.
We need a counteractive for
The past hour, when we opened up
The motor wide for home, because
The day drew tight with rain. Riding
Squeezed tight away from icy clothes,
Seeing the downdrawn vegetable,
Fancying the indrawn animal
Along the shore, we seemed to know
Contraction is a movement in
The pain direction, the fanged clutch.

On slaty riding waves that ride
The lake, some brown mergansers ride
Down near the rock shore. They look pert
And pleased under the rain and wind.
When the lively flock has drawn too tight,
They do what flocked mergansers do:

Run on the water, spraying out
To make each bird more water room
On slaty waves. Thus expanded,
They settle, looking pert and pleased.

III

THE CAVEMEN AND THE PHONOGRAPH

I who address you
Am descendant of the child of four
Who was told that once there were cavemen.
Told any edges or weights
To shape him the shape of cavemen?
Maybe he made that later.
(I made that later.)
But he burst out crying
Because he couldn't be a caveman.

His father told him
That, if he *had* been a caveman,
He couldn't have listened to the phonograph.
No rolls of nice gooey sound
To spin in his head and his stomach
—He *did* love the phonograph.
Yet it couldn't console him
For being no caveman.

II

Sits firm on sun-warm stone
With his heels and his calves
Taking the solid and the scratch
Of sun-warm stone
—That's what a caveman does.
And under the hard of his fingers
Is the hard of a bone,
A big, bare, yellowed bone.

His eyes are clear, and his forehead clear,
Because he need not try
To find coefficient words
Of sitting there where he sits,
Or words to name his concern

With basic sun, stone, bone
—Eyes pure as stone, forehead smooth as bone.

III

Tum, tum-tum, tum-tumpty, tum-tum
—The barcarolle, wasn't it, from *Tales
Of Hoffman?*
And it was, whereas cavemen were not.
And it was: word without sharpness,
Smoothing, cream-feeling sound
To undulate with him
So sweet, so liquid sweet.

But—rasp, jar . . .
Wasn't there something afloat
On the honeyed undulance?
Wasn't there mention of a boat?
Then where were the sun-worn, water-worn fibres,
The paint flecks losing hold,
Of the boats that are?
Where were they? Where were they?

IV

Descendant,
(Says the boy-ghost),
Thing-lover,
You make images out of words.
Could a caveman live on word-made images?

I am faithful
(I grumble)
To my genealogy.
Those images, maybe, are my tears for cavemen.
I have shed them and shed them.
Listen:

V

Snowy hills, covered with black spruce.
One could assume the snow.
That the spruce was, largely, black spruce
—Well, a book said so.
One could assume the nail marks
Where, in the snow, in icy nights, would go
The quadruped lords of that creation.
(Anyhow, books said so.)
And that was New Brunswick.
And I was going to burrow deep into it
Like a humbler Thoreau
(Even if I hadn't heard of Thoreau.)

The time my remote, minuscule homestead
Had really the weight,
The firmness to support me
Was the time when, out in the yard,
I trimmed and whittled a stick
Of ordinary willow.
One could certainly use such a stick
As some small tool, some replacement,
In his shack far hidden in the snow
Of New Brunswick.
Exactly what tool, I didn't know.
But it was so.

VI

Because I can't touch you or see,
Only speak of the place you are,
Vaguely,
Using words like obscure
And murky and gloomy
And remote, down far,
Out of reach surely
Deep in the dark, dreary, eerie
(Might as well be Poe/nevermore),

57

I charge you, walleye, bite!
Slosh the top water white!
You may bloody my hand with a dorsal spine
As I lift you aboard.
The blood will be worth it
To touch the rough of your scales,
To see your cloudy-grape eye,
To see your yellow, black, orange; and see
The edging of purest white
On the lower sweep of your tail.

VII

Call them tears then.
And say tears are thingy.
Yet they can't float a boat,
Neither seat a caveman.
They're not my favorite things
(Says the boy-ghost).

Here's a stumble!
So things won't support us, automatically,
In happy, no-word equilibrium?
They're not all one soul-size?
They may let us down?
(I grumble).
Very well, I'm genetically loyal:
I can stub my toe too.
Watch:

VIII

A cat, unmistakable black house cat,
Scampered scat scat.
And I thought, "What's he doing in this empty range,
This setting for the coyote and the jack rabbit?
Kind of nice, though: he must be making it,
And wherever something is able to fit, let it fit."

58

And I thought, "No, damn it, his right is forfeit.
When his millionth grandmother took to the milk and the fire
She renounced cat claim
To fieldmouse and meadowlark. Now it
Is not good strange but bad strange
To see this descendant feral on the range.
Cat thing is not cat thing as it should be.
I cannot see it happily."

IX

The muscles back of my ears draw tight.
The ears draw close to my head.
I might be a cat or wolf
Ready to fight.

All right;
More fang power to cat or wolf.
But these are *my* ears; what are they doing
Ferally drawing?

X

Thing
Becames memory
Becomes word.
Yet word
Is from memory
Is from thing
(I grumble).
Would it be cheating
If I just invoke Logos St. John
And Beginning/ Word/ God
Which must be as fibrous
Warm scratchy hard
As thing?

I'm sleepy
(Says the boy-ghost).
Some words are useful.
I can rock me to sleep, if I want to,
On the honeyed undulance.

THE FIREWEED

I

Thomas Hardy would
Have given ten years of his life to see a ghost.
Poor doubting Thomas, he would see a sign;
But, from where he stood,
The signs of his times pointed to dust.
And yet, what kind of life-sign would that have been
If he had seen it, some gibberer in corrupted Gothic,
Flapping like tired laundry?
Crude, crude.

My grandfather (biological)
Said once, "*That* is a ghost
If there are any; and if it is
I'm going to catch it." Then without the least
Trouble he slipped up and grabbed with his broad,
Muscular hands a squawking fellow who stood
In a night hallway in a white nightshirt.
Crude, crude.

II

I'm so weary of Whitman, who couldn't even tend a lawn
For a minute or a page
Without showing that his place-time-direction
Was future-up, not now-down.
He says that his grass is dark; I think it got so
By soot and char from his flying-saucer blast-offs
Into those high mists whence cometh never a checkable answer.
He is like those scientists with the future in their bones;
They'll die of bone cancer.

III

"We are all descended from grandfathers."
The guidebooks are outmoded. The vermiform appendix a nuisance.
Yet we are all descended from grandfathers.

"Descended" suggests something; it mutters "gravity."
"Gravity" suggests something; it mutters "fall."
When you fall, what control?
Where my ancestors muddled, shall I escape crudity?
In the grasp of grandfather gravity, all
(Though they soar like ghost or like bard)
Shall follow the old course down
To their verdant earth; and use it probably ill;
And use it to bounce on.

IV

And father Frost spoke of synecdoche,
And that meant an oven bird
Singing of men and of God
Without singing.
Oven birds nest on the ground.

V

Suppose a man gets chosen by
A ground term, sweet vegetable thing from the ground,
As the visible node of his metaphor.
His emotions will smother up to it like dodder.
Won't they end by tangling a messy cover
That blurs out identity?

At any rate, parasites know their hosts.
(Have you gathered mistletoe from cornstalks lately?)
They even humbly declare
That their clinging affirms the name
Of the host they cling to; and it lives beyond them,
Lives on when they disappear.

VI

(Or put it:
Who cares at all for the flapdoodle gauds
Compared with the cool grace, the green
Of the north-grown fir twigs they hang on?
But they do assert there's a Christmas tree.)

VII

We can't make it like foxes or otters.
Living unwrapped in their brush or water
—Chop off; the comment is apparent.

Cased in our polyethylene bags
With vision obscured by the fogs
Of our reused breath and our tears,
We peer out, and blame
This plastic return to the womb.
Isn't it better outside?

When Christ the devourer comes,
What if he comes in the guise
Of those tough-gutted microbugs
Some laboratories look for
That will live by devouring plastic?
Won't it be better outside?

VIII

Out there, up north,
The fireweed blooms.

In Michigan, Minnesota I never noticed it much:
I believe that it must stand taller, brighter,
With every degree toward the pole.

Not fire-colored
It connects with fire:

Against long flame-blackened spruce miles
Below Great Slave, maybe, or Lesser Slave,
It centers and points whole landscapes
As though from the mastering fire
It had taken mastery.

Not at all blood-colored
It connects with blood:

" 'When the fireweed blooms, the moose have most fat on them'.
That's what they say in the Yukon.
When the fireweed blooms, then they shoot them."
Word of a hitch-hiker from the mines around Yellowknife.
Image of heavy, rich blood
Gouting across those blossoms.

IX

Think of the red man.
Not at all fire-colored,
He connects, you could say, with fire
In the sense that he got burnt down.

Stalks of fireweed lighted the growth
In the northern Saskatchewan cemetery
That bore this bloom of found poetry
Trellised above its gate:
"If we could not as brothers live,
Let us here as brothers lie."

X

A shabby theatre, partially filled
By me, and some poor dim-witted zoophile,
And an African documentary.
Jungle, antelope, pigs.
Sweating black skins, nets, brave dogs, spears.
Behind me the poor dim-witted zoophile
Shrilled,
"O, it will only be killed!"

Her companion or keeper would have instilled
Some sedative lies (or truths, conceivably)
Re need, and selectivity, and restraint.
But the poor dim-witted zoophile
Wouldn't be stilled:
"O, it will only be killed!"

If a person has got quilled
By fears that work in like the pines of a porcupine,
He needs more than sedative lies or conceivable truths.
Draw out, draw out!
I need now the drawing power of the ground
Out there, up there,
Because periodically I rattle inside me a refrain
Not willed:
"O, it will only be killed!"

XI

"Alive and well somewhere."
But the sign, the sign?
I carry an uncomfortable bloodline.
Stand on the right ground before
You can bounce up, out of fear,
With Whitman.
Shifting, shifting . . .

XII

Gnaw at it as you will, you'll only break your teeth:
There's no constructing without destroying,
And the made is seldom as good as the unmade.

XIII

That area which produces most human food
Produces automatically
Most human excreta.

XIV

A rich red drift on the prairie:
Those fragrant and lovely wild strawberries.
"We'll go there this afternoon."
But a farmer came with his gashing plough
And his slow, smashing team;
And many things had their rate of change
Speeded. There were
No strawberries left that afternoon.

And the poor old appeaser who told me about it
Laughed at his distant, littleboy tears.
There had to be wheat, didn't there?

These days, the trailed clouds
Are pretty well lost in the smog.
But on that old day, they reflected
A principle back to the earth
One may translate thus: In the vision
That the fireweed guards
It is known that the only use
Of the useful is support of the useless:
Never for the sake of wheat
Is there wreck of wild strawberries.

XV

Most people, of course, are than-thou's:
Reality is their buddy more than thine.
(Regard the smugness of eye, the slant of nose.)

Exempli gratia:

Engineer/technician who can move
Better than thou the planet's solid matter,
And could easily give thee too a shove.

66

Holy man, master of lotus position which
Would rack too harshly thy cumbrous joints,
Who will rise to the One, leaving thee in the fecund ditch.

Hardhat/armored athlete who can endure
Harder blows than thou, thereby ring from Truth
Notes than thy poor dinging more sweetly pure.

Poet/novelist whose command of the nitty
Is grittier than what thou canst declare,
Who speaks thus a whiter rage, a blacker pity.

And always the self-gratulatory young
Who cry, "I am more I than thou!"
Leaving thee bemused at whom thou walkst among.

The fireweed is prettier than those.

XVI

As you engage the world,
The dread that it must draw you in
With all those Hindu-god tentacles
And engorge you, will lead you
To try to engorge the world.

What error, how crudely too big!
You feel so swollen!

It didn't seem my creation;
But there leaped into mind, and remains,
A picture
Of a purposeful cottontail rabbit,
Alive, warm, springing
Through frosty grass in a pasture
Toward a leafless blackberry thicket.

Follow the rabbit, obese one,
Over fallen blackberry leaves
Down his run between thorny stems,
Tight under thorny tangle.

You'll emerge lean and running.

XVII

Honest ancestor, skip it.
Though I mentioned a rabbit,
Bunny has not nibbled down the fireweed.
I never said grabs of the senses
Were interchangeable.

At 15, hot age, I lay awake in the moonlight
And watched the moon dapple and dapple
With moon coins and moon bars the leaves and the earth;
And heard the wind heighten and lessen
Its murmur in twigs and in weed stems;
And smelled the variety of earth;
And suffered a beauty of a toothache.
And I said out loud,
"The only reality is pain."

This is a useful recollection.

XVIII

(As for the rabbit: after long running,
He may find a form
Under the fireweed.)

XIX

Caught in the bleaks and drears
Of insomnia, have you tried forming
A steady image on the long, uncolored
Reaches of night? The personal will
Can't manage: the picture falters,
Demeans itself out; the engorging general
Reigns. (He should have meant this,
The sad initiate who said that three in the morning
Is the hour that condenses the whole dark night of the soul.)

68

XX

Thomas Hardy could
Make a little hop-bounce occasionally
And, being briefly in the air,
Surmise in thrush or ox comforting awareness
Of which he was unaware.
But propellant and surmise failed; he came thud
To the ground, to remain honestly, honorably
Sad.

Whitman did
Occasionally stub his toe on the take-off:
Wasn't everything flashes and specks?
Yet established his airy balance
To speak with assurance
Of limitless mullein or mossy scabs on the worm fence
Or miraculous mice; and remain
Mistily glad.

My grandfather (biological)
Died saying firmly
In the French of Quebec and his boyhood
That something was a very good bargain.
To whom he spoke, or what was a bargain,
He never said.

XXI (Coda: To One Dead)

I'm in the old place, a long way south of the fireweed.
But the prairie ground is doing pretty well this June.
The path's just a trace, the sweet clover has grown so high,
And all up the hillside is a round sound blooming
Of wild rose and coneflowers. Flickering lake light
Counterpoints the flickers rebounding from the smooth
Cottonwood leaves.
   Et cetera. I wouldn't call you back.
Better there, better now. This is mostly just to say
That though not too cheery, I'm making it not too badly;

And to ask, if this gets through to you in your range,
One small piety: from some leaf adjacent
To the mastering bloom, could you hang it like a Christmas gaud?